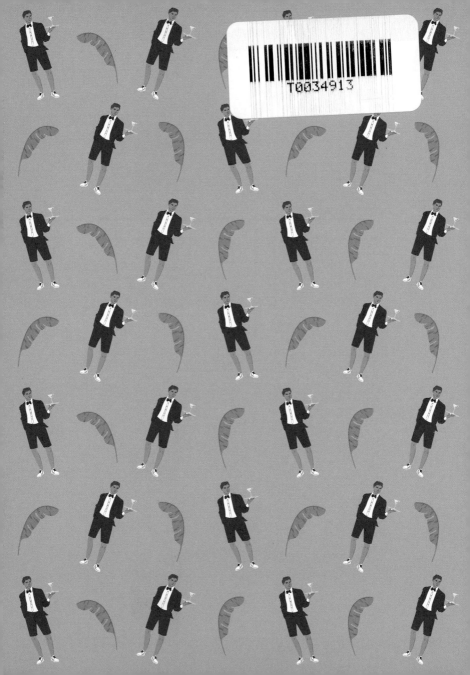

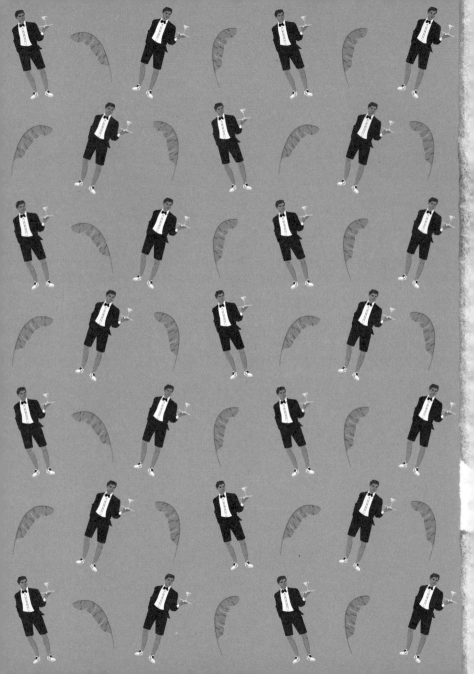

THE MANSERVANT GUIDE TO MODERN CHIVALRY

Every Woman's Fantasies for the Men in Her Life

Dalal Khajah & Josephine Wai Lin

Illustrations by Kine Andersen
Design by Jessica Hägg & Sadie Williams

Simon Element
New York   London   Toronto   Sydney   New Delhi

SIMON
ELEMENT

An Imprint of Simon & Schuster, Inc.
1230 Avenue of the Americas
New York, NY 10020

First Simon Element hardcover edition April 2024

SIMON ELEMENT is a trademark of Simon & Schuster, Inc.

Simon & Schuster: Celebrating 100 Years of Publishing in 2024

For information about special discounts for bulk purchases,
please contact Simon & Schuster Special Sales at 1-866-506-1949
or business@simonandschuster.com.

The Simon & Schuster Speakers Bureau can bring authors to your live event.
For more information or to book an event, contact the Simon & Schuster
Speakers Bureau at 1-866-248-3049 or visit our website at
www.simonspeakers.com.

Manufactured in China

10   9   8   7   6   5   4   3   2   1

Library of Congress Cataloging-in-Publication Data has been applied for.

ISBN 978-1-6680-1251-2
ISBN 978-1-6680-1252-9 (ebook)

To our ManServants, for
making our daydreams a reality

INTRODUCTION

Hello, my lady. I'm here to fill your cup with rosé, massage your neck after a long day, and feed you fries as your manicure dries. Your burger is on the grill, just the way you like it. Don't get up. I've already taken out the trash. And by the way—have I told you today how beautiful you are?

Question: Why do these images make our ovaries explode? And why have we created a company called ManServants to offer chivalrous services to women?

Because we women are exhausted.

Right now, we're running the world, and it's about time, but it's a lot. We crave reciprocity in this game to help carry the load that is life—a team player, a value-add, someone just as powerful as us.

Ladies of leisure* of today want to meet their match. The Mark Antony to their Cleopatra. The Jean-Paul Sartre to their Simone de Beauvoir. The Barack to their Michelle.

But how do we make this happen? What do we, elusive ladies of leisure, want, exactly?

———

*This book was written from a cis female gaze, but we also intend for "men" and "women" to be interpreted as performative roles that can be played by either gender.

CHIVALRY
IS
~~DEAD~~
CO-ED

WHAT DO WOMEN REALLY WANT?

ManServants started as a joke, and then it became real. Back in 2014, "selfie" had just been added to the dictionary, and we released a promo video declaring "What Women Really Want," featuring hot gentlemen catering to every whim and fancy. And it went viral. A quit-your-day-job-and-dedicate-yourself-full-time-to-being-Millennial-Madams kind of viral. This pivot into accidental entrepreneurship gave us front-row tickets to a social experiment of our own concoction and an antidote we needed to share with the world.

ManServants, the company, was born when we realized not all women liked a penis rubbing against their face for their last-hurrah-of-freedom fantasy. So we founded a company that trains* and delivers dapper gentlemen to serve as party entertainment and fulfill our clients' nonsexual fantasies. We began by asking our clients how they wanted to be treated. We didn't realize at the time we were building the largest database of women's nonsexual fantasies. (Okay, Google and the NSA have us beat, but our way sounds cooler.)

Our most surprising finding was that no one had really asked women what they wanted before. Male fantasies exist all around, but when it came to bachelorette parties and

---

* Words like "servant" and "train" may trigger some people. When we use the word "training," we're referring to our prospective employees, and a training program is standard for onboarding. The term "servant" simply refers to someone in service of someone or something. Like our company name, it should be taken tongue in cheek.

beyond, we realized our entertainment options were hand-me-down fantasies from men.

Even the Code of Chivalry, a medieval ideal for how to be a gentleman and respect women, was written by knights who had the *gall* not to consult a single dame.

It didn't take long for us to notice we were onto something. The front-row seat a ManServant gets at one of our events is rare. They get to witness a group of women with lowered inhibitions doing whatever they want, declaring their love, checking in, and spilling confessions with every chug of prosecco. It's not a pillow fight, but it's a fantasy made real nonetheless.

We once had a ManServant describe this anthropological experience: "Don't get me wrong, I hang out with girls, I'm comfortable with girls, but I had no idea . . ." (As women, we had a good idea of how our clients behave—it's no knitting circle.) He was in awe. He had discovered the land of women.

So how did our ManServant get there? Did he perform some trick?

A generic compliment? Nope. He achieved the ManServant state of mind. This transcendental state allows our clients to feel at ease in his presence; they don't feel judged, so they reveal their true, sparkly natures. Their boundaries are respected, so they feel free to release themselves from accountability, responsibility, and all the other boring -ity words. A ManServant cuts through the surface pleasantries with a cake knife, transforming our clients into ladies of leisure.

It didn't feel right to us to have this secret formula or charge a premium for it. With this manual, we hope to deliver all the lessons that have worked for us during our tenure of providing dream men. We hope that by sharing what has worked for us in the context of our company, we can give you the language to ask for what you want and know it's what you deserve. Our definition of true success is that no amazing human settles for mediocrity ever again.

GIVES
MASSAGES

KNOWS 3
LANGUAGES

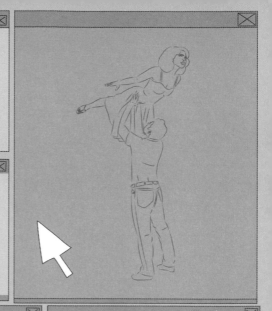

MANSERVANT

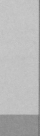

LOADING_

6.5FT+

TALL
DARK
PAMPERING

WHAT WOMEN REALLY WANT

98%

How to read this book
Our company caused a scene by flipping the
script on traditional gender roles like a Freaky
Friday. Through this live-action role-play come
the lessons that fill these pages.

Exhibit A
Traditional Gender Roles

MAN
TAKES CARE OF SELF

WOMAN
TAKES CARE OF OTHERS

Exhibit B
Gender Freaky Friday (i.e., our business)

MAN
TAKES CARE OF OTHERS

WOMAN
TAKES CARE OF SELF

With this manual, you have the power to turn people into ManServants, spot ManServants, raise ManServants, or become a ManServant. Take and make it your own. Use irresponsibly.

Choose Your Own Adventure
While most of our clients are women, anyone can be a lady of leisure, and everyone has a ManServant within.

MASCULINE SIDE

FEMININE SIDE

Masculine and feminine energies live within each of us. Like yin-yang principles representing the dualities in life, one can't exist without the other, but they aren't static parts. Our parts are not static, either. Being able to tap into all sides makes us more complete humans.

Drop a Hint
We've got some lessons for the men in your life, too. Feel free to leave pages of this book open around the house when you want them to get the hint. We have sections for Cocktails (page 39), Photoshoot (page 43), Compliments (page 71), Self-Defense (page 95), and ManServant for a Day (page 119). You're welcome, (wo)mankind.

the *ManServant*

In 2014, our version of a "dream man" was only that: a man who existed in our daydreams. He wasn't real, so we, the Ladies of ManServants, made him up.

Locked away in our proverbial start-up garage, we went on a word hunt to see if a term came close to what we were looking for. Turns out one does, but *philogynist*, which is "a man who likes or admires women," is too weird a word to use on the reg. There are, however, plenty of catchy words to signify a man who hates women, which include, but are not limited to: chauvinist, misogynist, sexist, woman-hater . . . Thank you, patriarchy.

The term "ManServant" has existed since the fourteenth century as an old-timey British phrase. Queen Victoria even had one at her beck and call by the name of John Brown. Their companionship aroused some suspicion, but who could blame a queen for appreciating a man who put her first? But here we're talking about a different kind of ManServant—one for the modern woman, sans the powdered wig. It needed a makeover, and we were the ones at the drawing board.

ManServants possess six attributes that make
them ridiculously discerning, which are:

Emotional Intelligence
Charm
Wit
Feminism
Showmanship
Easy on the Eyes

Man•Serv•ant
/'man,sərvənt/   *noun*
A chivalrous gentleman at your nonsexual service.
Used in a sentence: "Where's my ManServant?"*

* An official definition from Urban Dictionary, so obviously it's legit.

the Lady of Leisure

Whenever a ManServant suits up, a lady of leisure is born. When something needs attending to, he steps into action. A lady of leisure glances aloofly at that action and says, "No, thank you. I'm *le tired.*"

Finding your inner lady of leisure is an ancient right. It dates from the times of Cleopatra's posse puffing on opium in draped tents to noblewomen sipping high tea and ignoring the responsibilities of court—even God Almighty had a day of rest. Today, it's the ritual of looking at the items on your to-do list or your three-year-old's crocodile tears and making them someone else's problem for a change.

ManServants carve out free time for ladies to shake out of their roles. To enjoy a glass of wine with a friend, step outside to look at the moon, take a class, or get a manicure. It's the luxury of nothing without the guilt. They can also carve out time and support for the ladies to answer their emails or work on their individual goals because that's the secret to having it all.

These labels don't mean ladies of leisure are always women or ManServants are always men. Every fully rounded human is both a ManServant and a lady of leisure, depending on where their energy needs to go that day or hour.

Modern chivalry is mutual respect.

Old Chivalry

Is about power—controlling and subjugating women

Was written by old-ass cis white men

Supports superficial gender roles

Encourages grand physical gestures

Benefits the patriarchy and fuels toxic masculinity

Modern Chivalry

Is about respect—supporting and caring for each other

Is a collaboration between men and women

Supports gender equality

Encourages emotional intelligence

Benefits an inclusive society for all people

Chivalry needs a rewrite.

With old codes of chivalry missing a woman's perspective, we reinvented them. In the following chapters, we introduce a ManServant state of mind and new rules that benefit us all.

01—SERVICE

ACTS
OF
SERVICE
ARE
THE NEW

ACTS
OF
DERRING-
DO

ManServants follow up requests with an "As you wish." And it is precisely that—a wish to be of service. A ManServant chooses to provide acts of service freely, and the lady is willing to accept them in kind.

Servitude gets a bad rep, but everyone is in service to something—country, community, family, pets. It's the fastest way to make someone feel at ease. Women have understood this forever. After all, "acts of service" is one of the five languages of love.*

Giving comes down to motivation, which is making people happy, just because. IOUs or rectifying some balance of power is not what counts in relationships. As comedian Chris Rock affirmed in his standup special *Tamborine*, in a relationship, "you're both there to serve. You are in the service industry." When that happens, both cups runneth over.

ManServants offer their nonsexual services. It's a fantasy for whoever booked the event because they've planned everything up

---

* Gary Chapman invented and authored *The Five Love Languages*. The other four languages are words of affirmation, quality time, gifts, and physical touch.

until that point, and now they can let go. It's also a fantasy for the celebrant, who can be showered with the adoration they deserve.

We know from experience that our ManServants have discovered their motivations through events. Only through being of service will one notice its built-in rewards. Taking a good photo of someone, delivering a thoughtful toast, remembering to get more ice before it runs out, and making their favorite drink—these gestures unlock affection, trust, and appreciation. They've also been known to cause fluttering heart palpitations and sudden hotness, so take caution if performed while driving.

And the accolades will come. One time we had a ManServant shuck oysters for guests at a party. The guests reacted to this simple task as if he had composed a symphony of multiple orgasms.

When ManServants go above and beyond, our clients shower them with adoration, filling our inbox's "YAY" folder with variations on, "We LOVED Adonis!"

Make someone feel good, and they'll want you to feel good in return. That's the cute side of human nature. Energy and effort are often reciprocated, so if you're looking for more appreciation, or starting things off on the right foot, channel your inner ManServant.

Good acts of service are given often, given quickly, and appear effortless, even when they're not. That's because we live by the Golden Rule, and that is "To give is to receive."

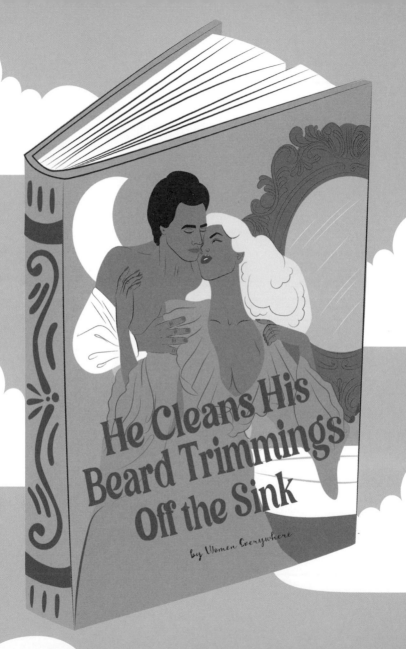

He Cleans His Beard Trimmings Off the Sink

by Women Everywhere

02—BOUNDARIES

WIT >
DICK

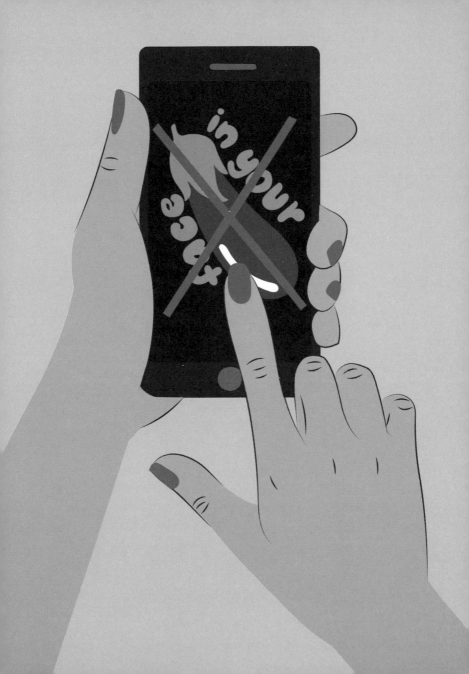

ManServants take a sacred oath to keep their tuxedos on, unless a lady beckons them poolside. When our clients hear this no-sleaze clause, they follow up with a "Yes, please" attitude.

Contrary to esteemed incel forums, this isn't because our clients hate sex. But when it comes to play with partners, color women cautious. When they first meet someone, they want to know boundaries will be respected before they get crazy, sexy, and cool. Too often, they are held accountable for everything from dancing around a creepy guy's feelings to the length of their skirt. We women will do anything to avoid the headline, "She Was Asking for It."

Our ladies of leisure want—nay, deserve—to lower their inhibitions with peace of mind regarding their comfort before perhaps indulging in their favorite vices. When suggestive comments, eyes, and hands are kept to themselves, both parties have time to figure out if they're speaking to an ax murderer or not. Win-win.

No matter how relationships evolve, the first step is to make a friend. This has notably been termed the "friend zone," an outdated notion invented by the Suffering Committee of Blue Balls, who base the value of female relationships on whether she'll give it up and, if so, how soon. Some men will spend years avoiding this zone, and the misogyny reads all over their personalities.

The friend zone is where the gold is. Men need more female energy in their lives and vice versa. Once men make it to the land of women, they can get advice on how to dress better, learn how to improve their game, get support when they need it, have someone who will listen when they're down, be introduced to cute friends, and get a self-awareness check when they need it, just like with your girlfriends.

It is easier for our clients to let their guard down with ManServants than with someone they just met because our service is born from boundaries. ManServants serve cheese plates, not penises. Ladies get to have their fun, and then *poof!* The ManServant leaves with their unraveled secrets kept to himself.

Restrictions may sound limiting, but ladies of leisure can't play unless they feel comfortable. In real life, boundaries shift as relationships progress, which is why continual check-ins are not only key, but sexy. These verbal agreements are what BDSM culture gets right. They've got the safe words, and everything else is fair game.

Our safe words are *no, stop*, and *Maroon 5*.

SHOW
~~OFF~~
UP

03—OFFERINGS

EMOTIONAL STRIPPING

"The need for massages is real.
I would pay for him to get training." —Alina

I magine you're expected to bring a hostess gift to an occasion every day, only you're broke as shit. That's being a ManServant. Every occasion is BYOO: Bring Your Own Offering.

Whether it's musical talent, arriving at a party with a ~~board game~~ bottle of tequila, making soup for a sick friend, proposing to make martinis for everyone all night, or washing all the dishes so the host can finally relax, offerings are how you put your best self forward.

When you think "ManServant," you may think "submissive," but this is far from the case. It's not enough to stand in the background, serving beefcake. ManServants always bring a social lubricant to a gathering. They serve thoughtful affirmations, curated playlists, a helping hand, interesting tidbits, culinary skills, or other unique talents.

While they do have alter egos, ManServants work with what they've got. For instance, they may take on the role of Mr. Rush, a man of mystery and a cocktail connoisseur, but this offering only works if they know how to mix a mean cocktail.

Some ManServants have apparent talents. Someone with a ballet background may offer the *Dirty Dancing* lift, and another with the voice of an angel may carry out R&B serenades. Still, grand or simple, all offerings are created equal.

Everyone already has plenty to offer. Even so, we live in the Matrix, aka the internet, where every potential offering is at our fingertips. Take a class, share your hobbies, learn how to keep plants alive, or offer a helping hand around the house. Round out your contributions, and we'll count you as one of the good ones.

And when all else fails, remember the best thing you have to offer is time and attention. That's a talent all its own.

COCKTAILS*

Through thick and thin, a ManServant always does the right thing. And the right thing is usually to ensure the lady has a drink in hand.

A ManServant knows how to make at least three drinks: his favorite; the lady's favorite; and one for whenever the lady may say, "Oh, I don't know, just get me something good."

On special occasions, ManServants make cocktails based on their guests' personalities or create personalized drinks themed for the event.

Presentation matters as much as taste. So put on a show as you mix, shake, artfully garnish, and then seal your offering with a toast.

*Kindly note that these are not original recipes. We, the Ladies of ManServants, have simply given tried-and-true recipes cute names. Never underestimate the power of presentation.

2 OZ GIN
1 OZ DRY VERMOUTH
LOADS OF OLIVE JUICE
OLIVES OR LEMON TWIST FOR GARNISH

Man Tini

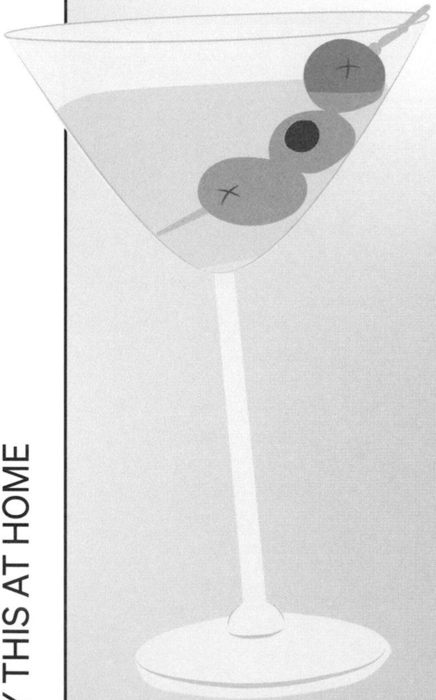

—

Add ice to a martini glass to chill. Add gin, vermouth, and olive juice with ice to a mixing glass or metal shaker. Stir, don't shake, for about 2 minutes. Strain into the chilled martini glass. Garnish with an olive or a lemon twist.

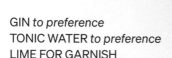

GIN *to preference*
TONIC WATER *to preference*
LIME FOR GARNISH

—

Chill a cocktail glass in the fridge
or with ice. Once chilled, add fresh
ice. Add gin and squeeze in juice
from one lime. Add tonic. Garnish
with lime.

Gent &
Tonic

2 OZ BOURBON
¾ OZ LEMON JUICE
¾ OZ SIMPLE SYRUP
ORANGE WHEEL OR MARASCHINO
CHERRY FOR GARNISH

Fuckboy Sour

—

Add ice to a cocktail glass to chill. Combine bourbon, lemon juice, and simple syrup in a cocktail shaker. Fill the shaker with ice, cover, and shake for about 30 seconds. Strain the cocktail into the chilled glass. Garnish with an orange wheel or cherry.

—

*A go-to ManServant move is to learn the lady's liquor of choice and then to invent a cocktail based on their personality.

PHOTOSHOOT

Acts of derring-do don't hold a candle to having a good photo of yourself. At our events, the lady plays the main character, and ManServants flock as the paparazzi. They've been known to construct human thrones to crown the lady under champagne showers to get the shot. Outside of events, the trained eye can always spot a ManServant out in the wild.

This rare specimen can be found squatting at the edge of a cliff with an optical zoom lens. At restaurants, they take photos of the lady outshining all entrées. They stop at nothing to capture the lady in the best light as she strikes a nonchalant pose against a historic landmark.

While beloved, this species of ManServant is on the brink of extinction, or simply lacks the skill set to capture a single flattering photo. We, as a society, must band together and put forth conservation efforts to nurture and protect them at all costs.

They say a picture is worth a thousand words, but if it's unflattering, it's best not to say anything. Here are some tips from our ManServants to get it right every time at the next gala.

———

Take photos when the lady isn't looking.

A fantasy for all ladies of leisure is to play muse
as a personal photographer captures their best
moments. Enter ManServants. Because to look hot
and have zero evidence of it is a cardinal sin at the
Church of Feeling Yourself.

———

Get on their eye line.

For the love of God, keep the camera just above eye
level. Women through the ages have learned that this
is our most flattering angle, and it's time you did, too.

———

Serve as arm candy.

Pull the lady into focus by looking at them adoringly
instead of facing the camera, give them a dip, or
incorporate props such as holding the lady's purse or a
fan to cool them off. Offerings look great in photos, and
it gives awkward hands something to do.

The paparazzi effect.

Make them the star of the show by waving off imaginary strangers as the lady struts down the street or exits a building, yelling, "No photos, please!" while a friend acts as the paparazzi to get the shot.

Follow the light.

No fantasy has ever come true under fluorescent lighting. Natural light is always a good idea, and the golden hour flatters us all. A good rule is to match the direction of the light source. Test by snapping the scene to see where the light hits best to determine the clearest angle to capture the lady. If shooting indoors without a lot of natural light, turn on the flash so the lady can edit better-quality photos later.

Play art director.

Be on the lookout for cute backgrounds and get extra credit if they go with their outfit. Exude patience as they experiment with different poses until they find their best angle. If they are out of ideas, you may suggest they gaze wistfully into the distance with our favorite pose, Looking for Your Imaginary Friend.

04—THE MENTAL LOAD

CARRY HER BAGS

PHYSICAL SERVICE

CARRY HER MENTAL LOAD

EMOTIONAL SERVICE

Picture this. It's Thanksgiving in the 1950s, and Mom is cooking a twelve-course meal while Dad has the game on and a timer set to baste the turkey. They've seemingly split responsibilities, but we all know this is a lie.

Mom is also thinking through what needs to get done for the house to function; she's playing mediator to passive-aggressive relatives; she's imagining all the things that can go wrong and making mental plans to prevent them from happening. If she voices concern, she's gaslit at every turn, or gets a comment like, "Relax, Nancy, you worry too much." All Nancy wants is for everyone to have a good time and will perform miracles to make it happen, but by all means, call her crazy.

Now let's fast-forward to today. Ladies have been diversifying their résumés. They're tuned in to their partner's emotional needs and bringing home the bacon. Nancy now works a full-time job but is still the primary caretaker of her children and household. She gets no credit when plans run according to schedule, and the emotional labor she invests into everyone's well-being is invisible yet always expected of her. The closest thing she's had to a self-care Sunday is reading the motivational caption on a toothpaste container while locking herself in the bathroom to escape little tyrants.

Nancy is our client; and to put it simply, she's ready to revolt. Her entire life has now become the party she has to plan. We call this *Hostess's Burden*.*

Allow us to illustrate.

———

*The Hostess's Burden is our spin on the Mental Load within the context of our company. The term "mental load" was first coined by French cartoonist Emma in her comic strip "You Should've Asked."

fig. 01

In the beginning, "man" used to signify
"provider," and "woman" indicated "caretaker."

fig. 02

Then one day, more than half the population showed up to work. With a word of encouragement from Destiny's Child, women can do it all now. They're independent and can earn a paycheck but are still often seen as caretakers first. Their household chores are gender-segregated, including the emotional labor it takes to make others comfortable and happy. Meanwhile, men's duties have remained relatively unchanged. This labor imbalance creates friction, and in the context of our company, we refer to it as the *Hostess's Burden*.

fig. 03

The hostess, as caretaker, goes where they are needed. They invite guests, bring mood boards to life, initiate introductions, insist they don't need anything but to see the joy on everyone's faces, and juggle the emotional work of meeting everyone else's needs—all done with a smile and likely while wearing something uncomfortable.

fig. 04

The hostess is an expert in giving. Their energy goes where it is needed, but when the burden of emotional and physical responsibilities falls squarely on one person's shoulders—their shoulders—it exhausts their chi. They want to channel their inner lady of leisure but can't keep up with the demands of an archaic system.

When duty calls, the lady wants a ManServant to rise to the occasion. Whether it's running out to get last-minute provisions, soothing a crying baby, or dealing with a demanding relative, a ManServant takes the reins, giving the hostess a much-needed break.

The hostess's brain will get a hit of dopamine from all the joy they're receiving for being able to kick back. They can put away the emergency Valium, bask in an abundance mindset, and live happily ever after.

The End

That's our little happily-ever-after story, but in real life, hostesses everywhere are still guzzling wine behind closed doors. We didn't realize when we conceived ManServants how important it is that we remedy the imbalance and make everyone aware of it.

The future can be coed, but reciprocity is the only way to get there. We refer to what goes down at our events as live-action role-play. ManServants step into the role that was traditionally monopolized by our women clients, and our clients get to manifest their nonsexual fantasies.

Role-play is sexy, and, it turns out, therapeutic.* Popular psychotherapist Esther Perel contends that role-playing increases empathy. It gives ladies of leisure a chance to ask for what they want and have a ManServant figure out the rest.

What Nancy wants is a ManServant, the antidote to the Hostess's Burden. As a tired woman once said, "It's God's gift to women."

---

*Psychodrama, an experiential method used in psychotherapy developed by Jacob L. Moreno, is when role-playing or role reversal is used to gain insight into interpersonal relationships.

PAY
THE BILLS
ATTENTION

05—MIND READING

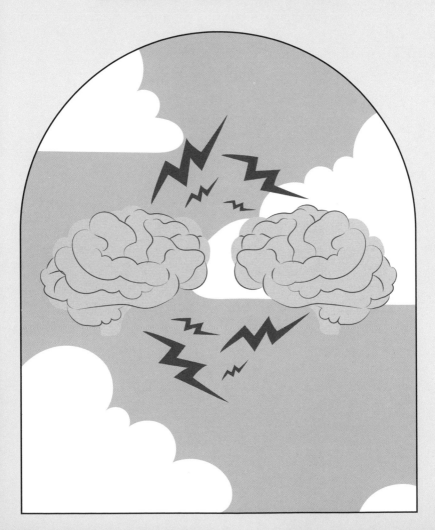

The lady is a strong, independent queen, like the late Supreme Court Justice Ruth Bader Ginsburg or drag queen Lady Bunny. They don't need their doors opened or to be waited on hand and foot, but ManServants want them to relax and enjoy themselves.

With ManServants, the lady is never in a state of want, and our clients pay a premium for that feeling. That's because, at some point in a relationship, they've heard something like, "Damn, Gina!* I can't read your mind!" yet that's precisely what the lady wants. Thankfully, mind reading is simple. The secret is to anticipate and approach.

How does one anticipate and approach? Well, by first doing nothing. The very first thing a ManServant does is read the room. He takes in the scene and assesses, "What could be better?"

A scene always calls for something. There is always something that can be fixed, thrown out, remembered, or improved, or someone to entertain before diving into a set plan or the couch.

Contrary to what inquiring minds may assume, our clients do not actually like to make requests. If a ManServant were to ask if they would like a refreshment, they would probably say something like, "Um, no, I'm okay. I don't need anything, but thanks!" They hate to feel like an imposition, or worse, a nag, but it doesn't take a weatherman to know the lady's parched under the scorching sun. So we at ManServants had to get creative with making sure their dreams come true.

---

*The catchphrase "Damn, Gina!" is courtesy of the TV show *Martin*, starring Martin Lawrence as the title character and Tisha Campbell as Gina.

The cheat sheet says if the lady has to ask, it's already too late. We tell our ManServants to read the room to anticipate what needs to get done and then do it without being asked. Because if the lady does ask, that means the request was already ticking away inside her brain, cutting short some hard-won leisure time. By the time most ladies ask for help, they're already at their wits' end and want solutions pronto.

We teach our ManServants how to mind-read by asking them, "What's wrong with this picture?" in everyday scenarios. If the lady's stressed at work, order them takeout or groceries for the week. If they've come home from running errands, take items off their hands. If it's about that time, pick up tampons. If the lady has a work call at home, take the kids out for an adventure walk. Suppose they reach for a joint—flick that Bic. If they hint at wanting more quality time, plan a date night.

This lesson is more of an art form than an exercise of clichés like opening the door. As all ladies of leisure know too well, what appears effortless is rarely that. When every scene is approached with fresh eyes, anticipating becomes second nature, which makes them a ManServant.

06—ADORATION

FILL
HER
GAS

GAS
HER
UP

EMOTIONAL STRIPPING

"I want him to be my die-hard fan, like be more obsessed with me than he is his favorite sports team." —Alexandra

Our clients are experts in caretaking, so it's unfortunate that that's what kills their lady boner. They are skilled at going where they are needed but wish to be wanted. When it comes to how they want to feel, our order forms are loud and clear: they want to be seen, adored, and, at times, objectified, but in, like, a respectful way.

ManServants play dream men, but the lady is the star of the show. Once the fog machine settles and the music cues, they use their screen time to give the lady their undivided attention. Giving anything your undivided attention may have been easy on the Oregon Trail, but technology and endless distractions have removed the sophistication of reading body language and the room IRL. ManServants know how to carve out quality time and put their phones away to notice the little details others may overlook.

By staying present, ManServants can shower their adoration in two ways. The first is with the art of compliments. A ManServant gases a lady up and empowers her to take on the world through words of affirmation and encouragement. "You're the shit" is a great start, but the best compliments are the ones that come from sincere observations, like noticing all the work the hostess has put in. Rest assured, we're debuting our Art of Compliments in this chapter. Feel free to leave the page open in the bathroom for your ManServant to get the hint.

Adoration is also shown through actions, the magnum opus of cinematic fantasies. Before events, we often give our ManServants a brief that lists the celebrant's favorite things, like their favorite song, so they may belt out a sneaky serenade in true heartthrob fashion. But most of the time, ManServants pick up those things during the event. It can be as small as taking the time to get a feel for their music tastes so they can pick the best playlist for them later. Or noticing a lady falling behind in the group and going up to them to offer an arm. It's often the simplest actions that speak louder than proclamations.

Gestures and affirmations make our clients feel seen. They often feel typecast in the roles they play from day to day, whether they're a caretaker, a parent, or a really good friend. All it takes is one person to notice and remind them they are also ladies of leisure. ManServants center the lady and let them shine because nothing feels as valuable as someone treating them like their story's main character.

"I feel seen when the guy I'm dating remembers when I have my first day of a big dance project and texts me good luck. Or knows my favorite kombucha flavor."
—Suzette

COMPLIMENTS

Does your neck hurt? It must, from carrying around that brilliant mind.

See, compliments (short of angels plummeting from the sky) are the most fun way to break the ice. Delivering a great compliment has a magical quality, like watching someone unwrap a gift you know they will love. Only it's free.

As a rule, ManServants never keep nice things to themselves. It takes empathy to notice the charming details in people. It takes a ManServant to say it with a wink.

Some compliments we hold on to like treasure, and we bet you can recall the best compliments you've ever received; all true, of course. Other times, they sound creepy. We once had a ManServant compliment someone's teeth at first sight, which was unforgettable, but not for good reasons.

When it comes to delivering a compliment, context is everything, and there is etiquette to ensure the utmost flattery.

THE ART OF COMPLIMENTS

1. Hand them out freely and give them often.

"You're the coolest person in the room."

—

Be attentive. There is always an opportunity to be flattering in context. *2.*

"Hey beautiful."
"Hey, beautiful. That outfit ought to be a crime."

3.

Pair compliments with introductions.

"This is Lulu. She sits next to me at work."
"This is Lulu—our go-to on all things tech. You should have heard the presentation she gave yesterday."

—

4.

Shower your guy friends with compliments. They're underserved in that department.

"You tell the story. It's funnier when you say it."

—

5.

Avoid comparisons or conditions because no one likes feeling measured.

"You look nice today."
"You look nice."

6. Avoid compliments around age. Being compared to yourself is even worse.

~~"You look great for forty-four."~~
"You give zero fucks what anyone thinks, and I need that attitude in my life."

—

Compliments on ability or behavior are more delicious than (unsolicited) compliments on bodies and appearance. *7.*

~~"Great ass!"~~
"You did that? What can't you do?"

—

8. Call out something specific to them to make them feel special.

~~"That's great about your raise."~~
"Of course, you got a raise. With your instincts, you'll be running that place in no time."

9. If you don't mean it, don't say it, but make a habit of finding the good in others and pointing it out.

~~"What an interesting story."~~
"It's inspiring how you can just go for it."

—

Accept compliments and resist the urge to give one in return immediately. It feels more genuine when you pay attention to the next opportunity (rule #2). *10.*

~~"Oh, stop."~~
"Thank you. That's nice to hear."

—

11. Gratitude is the highest form of compliment.

"A toast to you. I would literally be in a ditch somewhere if it wasn't for you."

07—EMOTIONAL STRIPPING

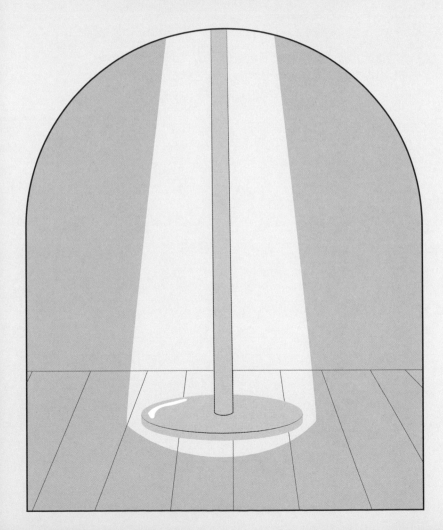

BE PRES ENT

IS THE NEW

BUY PRES ENTS

Conversation can feel like a lost art with DMs flooded with two-word questions, but good conversation is like dancing: it takes two to tango.

At our events, a typical female fantasy is something we call Emotional Stripping. Please allow us to paint with a broad brush here: a stereotypical hegemonic male fantasy is a striptease, while our clients are more interested in peeling back more emotional layers. They try to get a ManServant to break character with questions like "What's your real name?" "What's your backstory?" and "What's your relationship with your mom like?" To make connections, ManServants take it off emotionally.

To dazzle in conversation, ManServants lend an ear and make it about the lady. They break the ice, skipping the usual "How's your day going?" They listen to ongoing conversations, injecting interesting tidbits while following the rules of improvisation with a "Yes, and . . ." They answer personal questions and return them with a "But enough about me, tell me more about you." When the lady feels heard, it lifts the tempo.

ManServants must be able to make a connection with everyone in the room. To do so, they speak to the best version of a person (see page 75, rule #9 in our Art of Compliments section). To bring different groups of friends together, it's helpful to have one go-to question to find common ground and to reveal personalities. It can be an icebreaker like "If you had a theme party, what would the theme be?" or a silly question like "If you had to be a villain in history, which one would you choose?"

To avoid missteps, ManServants don't fight to control the conversation. They allow things to flow without being condescending, rude, or any of the bad. Instead, they keep it all-inclusive, sharing the floor and taking care not to step on anyone's feet by speaking on their behalf or interrupting them mid-thought. They give pauses to read between the lines. When someone is quiet, they ask, "What do you think?"

The back and forth, the building on what someone has said, the peeling away of layers—the dance of conversations creates real connections behind the fantasy. And those connections are fantasies all on their own.

"I want him to be as curious about me as Dave Letterman interviewing one of his guests." —Caitlin

08—ENERGY

BDE > COCKY

L et's be honest. Not all our events are Harlequin Romances made real. Especially in the early days of our company, there was trial and error and the occasional "This can't be happening." One particular lesson for us at the Dream Man Factory was when a client wanted our help realizing her perfect man. Back then, she could specify her type, and it read a little something like this:

- Acts like and knows everything about Teddy Roosevelt
- Must know ghost stories
- Tells me impressive facts about baseball games

Our ManServant had an hour to channel this character and carry out his Signature Service (cocktails, a photoshoot, compliments, etc.) while anticipating and approaching, all at a baseball game. It was a role that would have made even Tom Hanks seem schizophrenic. Needless to say, no fantasies were realized that day. We thought we were building a dream man, but it turns out we were building Frankenstein's monster.

He wasn't channeling the ManServant within; he was playing a role entirely outside of himself. We realized then that if he's going out of his way to make others comfortable, he has to start with himself. Since then, we've removed the option for clients to specify a type. We've found that his ManServant name and even his Signature Service all come second to the energy he brings to an event.

Ladies can forgive a bad fake accent or flopping on a good ghost story, but they will not forget how he made them feel. Our clients notice everything. They clairvoyantly read a ManServant's facial expressions, study his tone of voice when he's explaining that the penis-shaped ice sculpture has melted, and can tell when his body language seems dismissive. Their powers of observation would leave Sherlock Holmes out of a job. If ManServants aren't having a good time, our clients are unable to indulge in their fantasies.

A ManServant giving out compliments like Skittles is delicious, but his actual game plan is simple: walk in, curate an atmosphere, and leave the room better than you found it.

To help them get into the right mindset, we encourage Man-Servants to give themselves pep talks in the style of their favorite sports film or *RuPaul's Drag Race*. They may look like Adonis, but ManServants get insecure just like everyone else. These pep talks help boost their confidence and remind them to set an intention to make others happy. Things will happen beyond their control, but what they can control is to be calm and contained with whatever happens.

To accomplish this, ManServants put their focus on solutions, not problems. If a client is freaking out about the weather, a ManServant reassures them with, "The forecast does say it will be looking up soon, but I'll check to see if we've got tents."

When our ManServants are self-aware and have a healthy self-regulation process to roll with the punches, our clients become ladies of leisure.

09—SAFETY

SUPPORT ›

PROVIDE

To be in the presence of a ManServant is to be in good (and sexy) hands. That goes for the lady and the company they keep. After all, the bare minimum one should expect from a ManServant is that tragedy does not befall oneself.

ManServants walk on the side closest to the street and offer their arm to the slowest walker in heels. No one gets left behind and everyone gets home safely. This isn't because ladies are looking for a knight in shining armor, but any man who overlooks the safety of those around him is just another dragon.

Safety is an issue women and those in marginalized communities can't help but worry about. In the real world, they can't backpack alone across foreign lands, take shortcuts through the park at night, or meet a stranger without a healthy dose of caution. Longer routes, buddy systems, and turning on location services are all part of the female lexicon. To get to the land of women, ManServants must learn to speak their language.

More than a fantastic PSA on behalf of the transportation department, when ManServants see something, they say something. This may seem straightforward, but doing the right thing is easier said than done (note the bystander effect*). There is always a choice, and a ManServant is expected to make the right one. If a lady tells them something is up, ManServants believe her first and then investigate later. Whether it's a guy berating his girlfriend or a creepy dude on the subway, or the lady making her way down a dark alley to get to her car, they speak up, distract, tell someone, document, step in, or call for help.

Our clients want to have fun as much as the next person, but they constantly check in with each other. Having a ManServant around is additional reassurance that everyone is being looked out for. Safety becomes a problem that is theirs to solve as well.

Besides standing in the way of douchebags, unnerving situations, and fast-moving vehicles, ManServants are accountable for other people's safety. Only once the lady feels safe does play begin.

---

*The bystander effect is a social psychology theory that states individuals are less likely to help victims when other people are present.

SELF-DEFENSE

Hey, women aren't saints. We can change our minds, say the opposite of what we mean, and test limits as much as the next person. ManServants are skilled in the art of self-defense to escape those sticky situations. As any self-defense class will tell you, you're more likely to have to defend yourself against someone you know than a stranger.

There's always going to be a person who pushes boundaries. This person is easily identified at our events by yelling, "Take off your shirt!" This type of person is a problem at events. But ladies of leisure can smell bullshit from a mile away, so a ManServant rolling their eyes, being passive-aggressive, ignoring, or not providing a level of ease to that person is a big no-no. That's the opposite of charm.

Instead we suggest lightening the mood by using our favorite self-defense technique, which we call *Wit & Deflect*.

Wit & Deflect is when a ManServant uses humor and charm to de-escalate a situation and confuse the perpetrator. Some rare cases can't be redeemed and call for an emergency eject button, but mostly, there's always a graceful way to make an exit.

In the following scenarios, a ManServant would do well to employ the Wit & Deflect.

The Lush

A lady of leisure is too drunk.

—

A ManServant doesn't notice or draw attention to people's mistakes. The lady may feel foolish about it later, so laugh it off and let them know it's NBD.

Know that the lady is officially incapable of consenting to anything, so any game of Truth or Dare is officially off the table and real talk will have to wait. Grab them some water, make sure the lady gets home safely, and by no means leave them on their own.

"I'm Fine"

The lady seems upset about something, and you have a sneaking suspicion it's you. When you approach, the lady dismisses you with those fatal two words, "I'm fine." Spoiler alert: the lady is most assuredly not fine.

———

Saying "I'm fine" is the emotional equivalent of saying she doesn't need an umbrella in a monsoon.

Before jumping to conclusions, maybe it's not about you. Often a person just needs someone to make their situation feel easier at that moment. Provide an offering, then ask if the lady is okay. If they want time to think, offer them the space to do so.

But maybe it is about you. If so, go for the element of surprise. Defuse the tension with a massage or rapid-fire compliments until you get a smile. Don't stop until the lady expresses her needs.

The Damsel in Distress

A stranger is aggressively hitting on the lady.

—

The difference between a knight in shining armor and a douchebag is consent. Put down the sword and check with the lady first before stepping in with a rescue. She may define "dragon" differently.

The lady calls the shots on all things concerning her, and a ManServant provides the armor if they need backup. They provide an escape route, but it's the lady's choice if they want to take it or not.

If the lady wants to escape, be respectful to the stranger, disarm them with a compliment, and then usher the lady back to friends.

The Ass-umptions

You walk into a room. Maybe it's the kitchen, and you wrongly assume it's your wife's office by asking where your favorite mug is. Perhaps it's the office, and you invite your colleagues for a happy hour but exclude your female coworkers. Or it's a meeting, and you assume a man is in charge.

———

People are more than just one thing, and everyone plays a different role depending on the context of the situation or even the room. If you're at home, your wife is not the only caretaker of the house, so transition her role into a lady of leisure routinely and regularly. She may also be an expert in her professional field, even when double-fisting your child and a bottle. Your female colleague is not channeling her lady of leisure when she's at work. She's on the hunt for a promotion and would like to build relationships to advance her career.

It's up to the ManServant to gather information about each person's role at an event rather than resorting to reductive visual cues or internal biases. Allow roles to be fluid and interchangeable, as yours are.

The Advice Teller

The lady is venting.

—

When we complain to our girlfriends, the feedback is typically "Of course you're right, they're crazy." When we complain to men we get "Oh, I have the solution—this is what you should do."

We love guy advice, but most of the time we know how to solve the problem and just want someone to bear witness to our tragedy. Ladies need to vent, okay? This is the one time when being solution-oriented is not heartthrob behavior.

You do not need to fix or hold on to what the lady unloads. Lucky for you, empathy is easy—it just involves fewer words. Listen, validate their feelings, and when it's over, provide an offering to lift the mood. A cheese board is always a good idea.

The Nag

The lady is nagging you.

—

Just fucking do it.

The Bro

A dude jokes that his friend is "pussy whipped" because he's been staying at home with his girlfriend instead of going out drinking, or a boss judges a man for taking a month-long paternity leave. Both have small-dick energy.

———

This is less a self-defense method and more a piece of advice on how to navigate other men trying to control your relationships with ladies of leisure. Some men will always take the lazy way to feel superior.

Ask yourself why being at the service of others is cause for concern when the same concerned men often celebrate displays of toxic masculinity. Masculinity isn't something that should be re-proven at the expense of women. That's more the other word that also starts with *m*. We propose a new bro code in which guys support each other.

Laugh it off and lead by example. How you choose to define masculinity comes from within, not from other men.

OPEN ~~HER~~ DOOR(S)

10—THE NEW MASCULINITY

Masculine scripts read like old hand-me-downs. They're smelly, limiting, and often seem aimed at impressing other men, even at women's expense. Yuck. The pressures of being a man are real, but when masculinity is defined in opposition to the feminine, it's as toxic as *American Psycho*. In the sage words of Iggy Pop, "I'm not ashamed to dress 'like a woman' because I don't think it's shameful to be a woman."

The lady, and the world, will constantly challenge how open a ManServant is. They may say they're down for anything, but find out if they truly are at events. They never know what's behind closed doors. We've had a ManServant walk into what was detailed as a book club when—*surprise!* It turned out to be a smutty poetry reading. Kinky clients need leisure, too, and he commenced his Signature Service as per usual, albeit with a rather colorful dramatic reading. The rule is to always check judgment at the coat check.

One of our earlier codes was: A ManServant shall hold a lady's purse at her request, no matter how small, heavy, or sequined. This, of course, is more a state of mind than a general avoidance of lifting a finger. It lends itself to trying on lingerie as part of a bachelorette game, remaining stoic as they hold a parasol over ladies in front of confused strangers, mastering a hair braid, and carrying out a plethora of duties arbitrarily categorized as feminine.

They would be doing the ladies and themselves a disservice if they didn't approach these tasks with a "Cool, cool, cool" attitude.

Staying open to whatever comes their way tests how they choose to express themselves. As a result, ManServants define chivalry from what they've explored for themselves rather than something drafted by Don Draper.

It's easy to think masculine and feminine scripts have always existed, but we forget how much people have made up along the way.* These scripts control men as much as they control women.

---

* A bit of historical trivia for you: Men dominated the nursing industry back in the day. Then Florence Nightingale came along and declared, "Every woman is a nurse by nature." Overnight, it became a "women's thing." This happens a lot.

Activities get assigned by gender, and it's a stifling performance. ManServants flip that script.

The men who become ManServants in our company are naturals. They weren't "trained" to be gentlemen. They always were. They were comfortable with women taking the lead and turning the tables. All we did was add some panache and become super specific about communicating what we want. Maybe they haven't been as celebrated in the past, but ManServants are all around, in life and in our daydreams.

In our world, everyone's got a gentleman within, and everyone has an inner lady of leisure. The future is coed, and everyone should be opening doors for everyone. Masculine and feminine energies exist within each of us, and everyone's a swinger.

Following this rule won't turn men into women. It just means they'll slip into something a little more comfortable. *Bow chicka bow wow.*

YM
YOUNG AND MODERN
CRUSH TEST
READ HER SIGNALS
SOLVED
50 GIRL MYSTERIES
GIRLS BLAB ABOUT NOT CALLING,
THE L-WORD, AND LYING ABOUT SEX
IS SHE INTO YOU?
DONT TRY TO READ HER MIND - JUST READ THIS

LAST WORDS:
MAN-IFESTING

LITTLE DETAILS

OVER

GRAND GESTURES

Lessons from the Ladies of ManServants & how to achieve the ultimate fantasy

A question we've been asked countless times since debuting our cheekily named company is why we don't offer LadyServants. The obvious answer is that LadyServants have existed for all of his-story, but the second answer is that women already know what men want.

We, women, have spent our lives studying men: how to appeal to them, how to be agreeable, how to communicate through body language, how to say no the right way, how to be mysterious, how to make him think it was his idea, and so on. Thanks to the Patriarchal University of Life, ladies have done their homework.

Men, not so much. This is through no fault of their own. Like the rest of us, they went to the same university and "learned" what women really want from men. Or they learned from Pornhub. It doesn't help that women have been portrayed as painfully one-dimensional in various media, since they've been understood mainly through the lens of other men (see the Bechdel test*). To

---

*The Bechdel test is a measure of the representation of women in fiction. It asks whether a work features at least two women talking to each other about something other than a man. Newsflash: most films fail.

think there is nothing new men can learn from or about women is a lie also passed down by men.

We've come a long way since we first proclaimed ManServants as what women really want. We've vetted men in a style of *American Idol* meets Tinder, spent countless hours working in coffee shops amongst a sea of tech bros while men's abs adorned our computer screens, cry-laughed over order forms, and felt like actually crying when a ManServant failed to show. What started as a joke turned into something tangible and teachable. Our database of nonsexual fantasies has revealed that what our clients want most isn't to re-create a rom-com. They want the simple things.

Once, a client of ours, Chrissy, had a *Dirty Dancing*–lift fantasy, which we happily fulfilled. Later, she emailed us and said that for such a theatrical fantasy, what happened afterward was even better. She felt empowered to ask her boyfriend the same request. It surprised her when he eagerly said yes. She used her innate powers to ask for what she wanted, who she wanted it from, and playfully termed it man-ifesting.

Our clients want men to know how to be of service. When real life falls short on such archetypes, the fantasy of ManServants becomes all the more alluring—someone to walk in the room after putting out a fire and announce, "It's cocktail hour."

Contrary to what our company name suggests, our clients don't want subordinate men. They rarely opt for a butler role; they want a showman to tap in and take the reins, entertain when there's a lull at a party, and make sure no lady of leisure is left behind.

ManServants is tongue in cheek, and so much of what goes down in our events is about play. Our ManServants don't take themselves too seriously. While modeling lingerie gifts just for laughs, belting out a duet serenade, or showing up on the morning of a wedding and hilariously pretending to be the bride's long-lost lover, our ManServants are having a blast. It's likely because of these experiences in the land of women that most of our ManServants have been with us for years and often tell us they love what they do.

By stepping out of their existing roles, ManServants enjoy the satisfaction of being appreciated for their offerings and leave with a greater appreciation for what our clients do, which they bring into their real lives. We had a ManServant named Michael—whom we knew as McQuick, but chose Jacques as his ManServant name (are you following?)—tell us, "Being Jacques has taught McQuick a lot about what it means to be Michael." We completely understood and considered renaming him Confucius.

Admittedly, when we first promised to make "any wish come true," we were a bit concerned this would get us arrested. Turns out, the majority of the time our clients didn't want us to stage a kidnapping (although this has happened—it was very safe). Most often, they select a ManServant's usual Signature Service, served with some sexy emotional intelligence. Reading the room, anticipating, approaching, and the like is plenty fantasy for our clients.

It's their time to get the royal treatment, yet the most common feedback we receive is some remark like, "They looked like they were having such a good time!" or "He was such a good sport!" Even when it's their turn, our clients have more fun when their ManServant is also having a great time.

In return, our ManServants enjoy feeling needed, but our needs look different now than they did at the hands of patriarchy. White knights in shining armor to slay monsters come from the era of Damsels in Distress, but we are from the Age of Beyoncé.

In this new age of enlightenment, we propose rewriting your version of chivalry with your ManServant. The old rules of chivalry were not for us and rigged the game far before we stepped onto the scene. We believe in playing different roles and making our own rules, based on what we really want, which our ManServants may follow. And vice versa.

The ultimate fantasy is to give and take with no strings attached. This is what ManServants answers. We may know what it's like to receive, but not everyone knows how to give. This can be taught and ought to be if we wish to have reciprocal relationships with well-rounded, balanced, happy humans.

Whether it's making a dinner reservation, lifting heavy objects, or helping without prompt, everyone has a ManServant within that can use some polishing off.

The ManServant mindset is something to manifest on the daily. Only when we have the language to ask for what we want, with an air of entitlement akin to a sophisticated French lady beckoning *"Garçon!"* for more champagne, can we get it.

Women everywhere have the power to turn men into ManServants. And ManServants are waiting to be born. Our mission is to spread what has worked for us so we may render our business model obsolete.

One small step for women. One giant leap for mankind.

MANSERVANT FOR A DAY

The next time your boo asks you what you want for your birthday, Mother's Day, or just for a random Surprise Tuesday, here are a few ideas at your service.

The Short-Order Chef Itinerary

Plan an evening where you cook her anything she feels like eating that day. Let her sit down, kick up her feet, and tell you about her day over a negroni while you fire up the grill and get her favorite meal going. Bonus points for cleaning the house and doing some laundry to prep the scene for the big night.

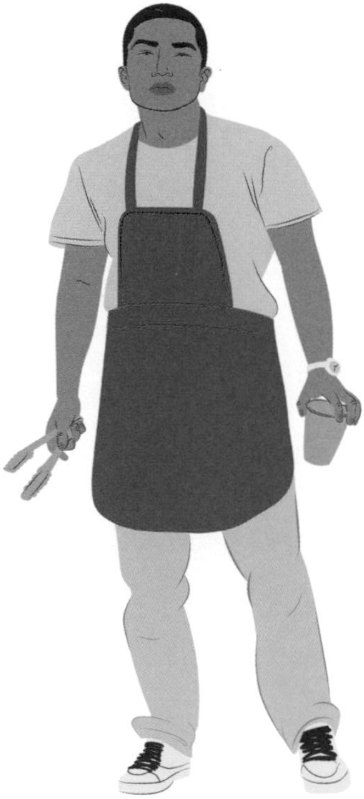

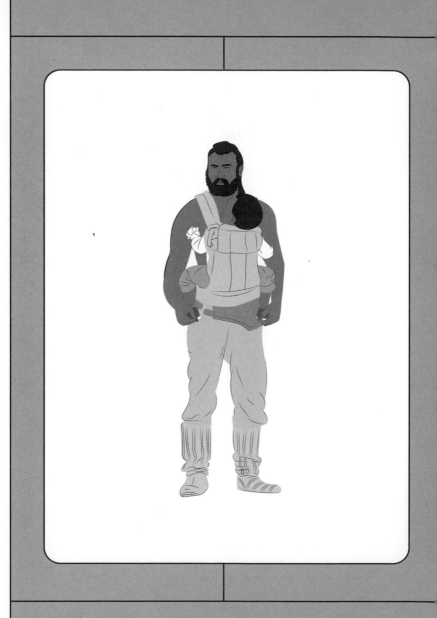

The DILF Zaddy Day

Take the baby off her hands for a day, a morning, or even an hour. It doesn't matter what she does with that time. She could work on her business, go to yoga, or sit in the car in silence. You happily take the kid and let her be kid-free, guilt-free, just f*cking free for a little bit. Bonus points for making this a routine, so she's not the default parent.

The Content-Taking Boyfriend Trip

Surprise her with a trip and then give the world THE RECEIPTS. Not because you are bragging but because you are OBSESSED with your girl. She looks bomb, and you cannot help but take super-flattering photos like you are her personal paparazzi. The key to this trip is preparation: listen to her and remember a place she wants to check out so you can make her mini dream come true.

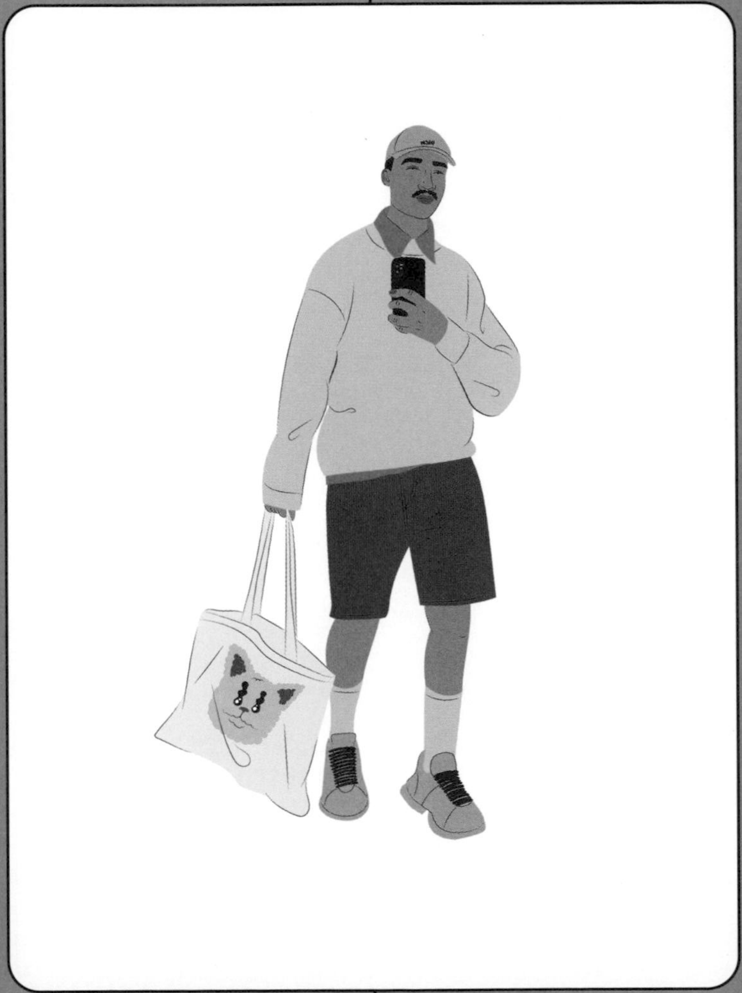

MANSERVANT FOR A DAY

TRY THIS AT HOME

The Welcome-Home Surprise

When she comes home from work, surprise her at the door with a bouquet of PUPPIES! Okay, okay, that would be morally irresponsible, but what other special something can you greet her weary, tired soul with? A cocktail? Reservations to her favorite neighborhood restaurant? Putting your phone away and being completely present during your time together?

OUR
GRATITUDES

Making this book has been a labor of love spanning over five years, the time it would have taken us to get PhDs in Women's Studies. Instead, we lived it. None of it would have been possible without the support of our families. At times, it appeared as though we were running a male brothel, and it's really cool that you supported us through it.

Mama and Baba, Nanay and Tatay, Elaina, Kyle, West, and Wolf, we love you, and thank you.

To Annie Pariseau for our "philosopher chats"; our extraordinary designer Jessica Hägg, who is always down to turn our crazy ideas into beauty; the ever-talented Kine Andersen, for the illustrations that splash these pages; Alia AlQimlass, for reading over every draft and believing in the vision; and Ali and Andrew Gilboard, for making the introductions to make this happen, thank you, thank you.

Our board of directors, J.P., and our investors Joyce, Curry, Eric, Mike, and John. Shout out to all the ladies of leisure who made this business a reality. Megan Kent, for constantly elevating us. Muneera and Gavriel, for all your pep talks. Lori, for being there for us every single day. Emerson, our Cutie Collector. Jen and Mickey for making our first video and all our videos.

And, of course, so much love and appreciation to all of our O. G. ManServants who are our Day Ones. You've made ManServants what it is today: Peter Clarkson, Simon, Kellen, John, McQuick, Will, Heath, Ajdin, James, Angel, VVH, Wolfe, Ben, and Kyle, whose biceps were forged from carrying Jo's mental load on the daily. You make us feel like absolute queens, and we won't stop until we bring that feeling to the world.

Clink, clink,

The Ladies

About the Authors

Dalal Khajah *is an entrepreneur, storyteller, and creative, and a co-founder and the COO of ManServants. She splits her time between New York and London, transforming ordinary men into dream men and running the blog* Majnoona, *which recounts dinner party conversations through a Middle Eastern lens.*

Josephine Wai Lin *is a creative director and entrepreneur, and a cofounder and the CEO of ManServants. She met her business partner, Dalal, more than a decade ago, when she was an advertising copywriter. Her first book,* Whoever You Are, *is a baby book about unconditional love and gender. After the pandemic, she left San Francisco for the slow life in Hawaii with her boy, Kyle (the first ManServant trainer ever), sons West and Wolf, and French bulldog, Drake.*

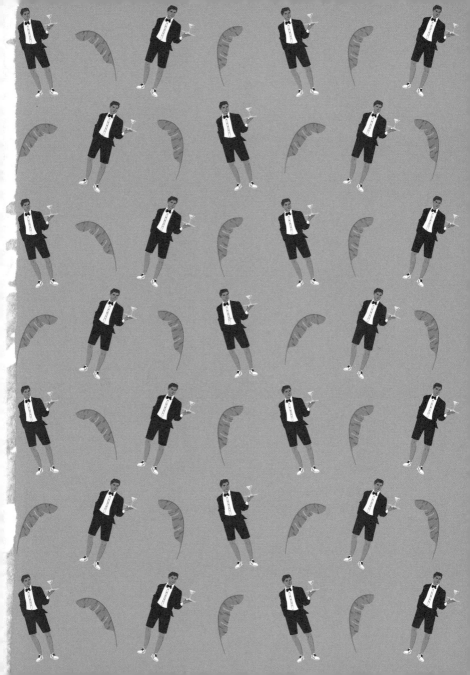

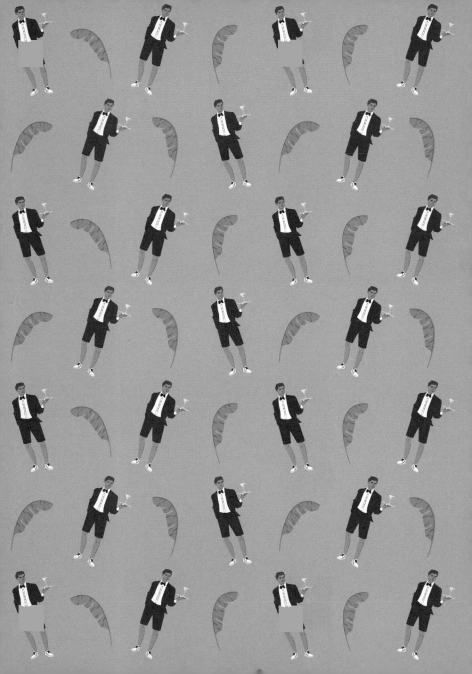